Scrum Master

Exam Guide and Certification Preparation

Table of Content

IMPRINT 3

1. ABOUT THIS BOOK 5

1.1. Introduction 5
1.2. Structure 5
1.3. Audience 6

2. QUIZ SCRUM THEORY 7

3. QUIZ SCRUM TEAM 21

4. QUIZ SCRUM EVENTS 35

5. QUIZ SCRUM ARTIFACTS 56

6. EXAM PREPARATION PSM 70

6.1. Exam Preparation 70
6.2. Exam Process 71
6.3. Sample Exam Questions 72
6.4. Sample Exam Answers 105

Imprint

2nd Edition 2020
ISBN 9781796766387
Copyright © André Dieninghoff

André Dieninghoff
Hainbuchenstraße 9
Germany - 44534 Lünen

This publication is protected by copyright. All rights reserved. The use of the texts and illustrations, also in part, without the written consent of the author is illegal and therefore punishable. This applies in particular to duplication, translation or use in electronic systems.

It should be noted that the software and hardware names used in the book as well as the brand names and product names of the respective companies are generally protected by trademarks or patents.

Professional Scrum™, Professional Scrum Master, PSM, PSM I, Professional Scrum Product Owner, PSPO, PSPO I, Scrum Open, etc. is the protected brand of Scrum.org. This book is neither endorsed by nor affiliated with Scrum.org.
All the content related to Scrum Guide is taken from scrumguides.org and is under the Attribution ShareAlike license of Creative Commons. Further information is accessible at http://creativecommons.org/licenses/by-sa/4.0/legalcode and also described in summary form at http://creativecommons.org/licenses/by-sa/4.0/.

This book uses excerpts from scrumguides.org official Scrum Guide from 2020. Scrum Guide licence:

©2020 Ken Schwaber and Jeff Sutherland. Offered for license under the Attribution Share-Alike license of Creative Commons, accessible at http://creativecommons.org/licenses/by-sa/4.0/legalcode and also described in summary form at http://creativecommons.org/licenses/by-sa/4.0/. By utilizing this Scrum Guide, you acknowledge and agree that you have read and agree to be bound by the terms of the Attribution Share-Alike license of Creative Commons.

Professional Scrum Master™ (PSM™), Professional Scrum Product Owner™(PSPO™) and Professional Scrum Developer™ (PSD™) are names, brands and trademarks of Scrum.org.

PLANNING POKER® is a registered trademark of Mountain Goat Software.

There can be no guarantees for the accuracy of the content. The information provided has been compiled to the best of our knowledge and beliefs as well as current knowledge.

1. About this Book

1.1. Introduction

If you want to prepare for the Professional Scrum Master certification the content of this book will help you. It imparts the knowledge needed to pass the PSM certification with first try because these questions can also appear in your exam. All questions and explanations are based on the current Scrum Guide from November 2020.

1.2. Structure

There are several questions including answers and the explanation to every Scrum topic. Furthermore, you will have a short guide how to prepare best for your exam certification. Additionally, you will have a sample exam at the end of this book so that you can already train your strategy for the real exam.

1.3. Audience

The main target group of this book are people who want to prepare for the Professional Scrum Master exam.

2. Quiz Scrum Theory

1. Who creates the 'Definition of Done'?
a) Scrum Master
b) Product Owner
c) Scrum Team
d) Development Team

Answer: d) The Development Team

Explanation:
If 'Done' for an Increment is not a convention of the development organization, the Development Team of the Scrum Team must define a definition of "Done" appropriate for the product. If there are multiple Scrum Teams working on the system or product release, the Development Teams on all the Scrum Teams must mutually define the definition of 'Done'.

2. Select the five Scrum values.
a) Openness
b) Courage
c) Commitment
d) Self-organization
e) Focus
f) Respect
g) Effectiveness
h) Agility

Answer: a) Openness, b) Courage, c) Commitment, e) Focus, f) Respect

3. What is shown by the 'Cone of Uncertainty'?
a) How much work remains till the end of the sprint
b) How much is known about the product over time
c) Hierarchy of tasks that comprise a project
d) Dependencies, start times and stop times for project tasks

Answer: b) How much is known about the product over time

Explanation:
The Cone of Uncertainty describes the evolution of the amount of uncertainty during a project.

4. Scrum is founded on:
a) Kanban system
b) Empirical criticism
c) Empiricism
d) Common sense

Answer: c) Empiricism

Explanation:
Scrum is founded on empirical process control theory or empiricism. Empiricism asserts that knowledge comes from experience and making decisions based on what is known.

5. Where do we use Scrum? Check all possible answers.
a) Development and sustaining of cloud and other operational environments
b) Managing the operation of an organization
c) Research and identifying of viable markets, technologies and product capabilities
d) Development of products and enhancements
e) Development of almost everything we use in our daily live as individuals and societies
f) Development of software and hardware

Answer: all answers are correct

Explanation:
Scrum has been used to develop software, hardware, embedded software, networks of interacting function, autonomous vehicles, schools, government, marketing, managing the operation of organizations and almost everything we use in our daily lives, as individuals and societies.
Scrum has been used extensively, worldwide to
- research and identify viable markets, technologies and product capabilities
- develop products and enhancements
- release products and enhancements as frequently as many times per day
- develop and sustain Cloud (online, secure, on-demand) and other operational environments for product use
- sustain and renew products

6. What is shown by the 'Burn-down Chart'?
a) How much work remains till the end of the Sprint
b) Dependencies, start times and stop times for project tasks
c) The evolution of the amount of uncertainty during a project
d) Hierarchy of tasks that comprise a project

Answer: a) How much work remains till the end of the sprint

Explanation:
Burn-down chart shows the evolution of remaining effort against time.

7. What is the meaning of the word 'development' in the context of Scrum? Select the best answer.
a) Development of an operational environment for the product
b) Product development, its releasing and sustaining
c) Software and hardware development
d) Research and identifying of viable market, technologies and product capabilities
e) Complex work that can include all the suggested options and even more

Answer: e) Complex work that can include all the suggested options and even more

Explanation:
When the words 'develop' and/or 'development' are uses in the Scrum Guide the refer to complex work including software and hardware development, development and releasing of products and enhancements, development and sustaining product operational environments, research and identifying of viable markets and technologies and even more.

8. What is the essence of Scrum? Select the best answer.
a) A small team of people that is highly flexible and adaptive
b) The Scrum Guide
c) The Development Team
d) The Scrum Master and the Product Owner

Answer: a) A small team of people that is highly flexible and adaptive

Explanation:
The essence of Scrum is a small team of people. The individual team is highly flexible and adaptive. These strengths continue operating in single, several, many and networks of teams that develop, release, operate and sustain the work and work products of thousands of people. They collaborate and interoperate through sophisticated development architectures and target release environments.

9. **'Definition of Done' is created in the first Sprint and cannot be changed until the final product release.**
a) True
b) False

Answer: a) False

Explanation:
During each Sprint Retrospective the Scrum Team plans ways to increase product quality by adapting the definition of 'Done' as appropriate.

10. **It is a good practice to sometimes have a special technical Sprint that consists only of tasks removing the technical debt without implementing any new functionality.**
a) True
b) False

Answer: b) False

Explanation:
The purpose of each Sprint is to deliver Increments of potentially releasable functionality that adhere to the Scrum Team's current definition of "Done".

11. **How often should Scrum users inspect Scrum artifacts and progress towards a Sprint Goal?**
a) Frequently, but it should not get in the way of the work
b) As frequently as possible
c) After the Daily Scrum
d) At the Sprint Review

Answer: a) Frequently, but it should not get in the way of the work

Explanation:
Scrum users must frequently inspect Scrum artifacts and progress toward a Sprint Goal to detect undesirable variances. Their inspection should not be so frequent that inspection gets in the way of the work. Inspections are most beneficial when diligently performed by skilled inspectors at the point of work.

12. **Is it normal to have a 'hardening' Sprint to remove technical debts and prepare the product for the next release.**
a) True
b) False

Answer: b) False

Explanation:
No, it is not normal to have such a 'hardening' Sprint. Development Teams deliver an Increment of product functionality every Sprint. This Increment is usable so a Product Owner may choose to immediately release it. Each Increment contains only 'Done' functionality that could be released immediately.

13. All the Scrum Teams working on the same product should have the same Sprint duration.
a) False
b) True

Answer: a) False

Explanation:
Scrum does not require having aligned Sprints for multiple teams.

14. What should be taken into account for the 'Definition of Done'? Check two possible answers.

a) Definition of Done of other Scrum Teams working on the same product
b) Conventions, standards and guidelines of the organization
c) Experience of the Product Owner
d) Definition of Done of other Scrum Teams working on other products
e) Advice of the Scrum Master

Answer: a) Definition of Done of other Scrum Teams working on the same product, b) Conventions, standards and guidelines of the organization

Explanation:
If 'Done' for an Increment is not a convention of the development organization, the Development Team of the Scrum Team must define a definition of "Done" appropriate for the product. If there are multiple Scrum Teams working on the system or product release, the Development Teams on all the Scrum Teams must mutually define the definition of 'Done'.

15. **The Sprint is cancelled if an item in the Sprint Backlog cannot be finished by the end of the Sprint.**
a) True
b) False

Answer: b) False

Explanation:
The Sprint is cancelled only in the case if the Sprint Goal became obsolete. If some work could not be done the Sprint Backlog should be re-negotiated between the Product Owner and Development Team.

16. **In Scrum only those Scrum components and rules which fit most for a particular project should be used.**
a) False
b) True

Answer: a) False

Explanation:
Each component within the Scrum framework serves a specific purpose and is essential to Scrum's success and usage.

17. What is Scrum?

a) A framework within which people can address complex adaptive problems, while delivering valuable products.
b) A software development methodology which is intended to improve software quality.
c) A sequential design process, uses in software development process, in which progress is seen as flowing steadily downwards.

Answer: a) A framework within which people can address complex adaptive problems, while delivering valuable products

Explanation:
Scrum is a framework within which people can address complex adaptive problems while delivering valuable products.

18. When must an adjustment be made ff an inspector determines that one or more aspects of a process deviate outside acceptable limits?

a) As soon as possible to minimize further deviation
b) After clarifying all the details with the Product Owner
c) The deviations should be discussed at the Daily Scrum and then an adjustment must be made
d) After Scrum Master approval

Answer: a) As soon as possible to minimize further deviation

Explanation:
If an inspector determines that one or more aspects of a process deviate outside acceptable limits and that the resulting product will be unacceptable, the process or the material being processed must be adjusted. An adjustment must be made as soon as possible to minimize further deviation.

19. Scrum is neither a process nor technique. True or false?
a) False
b) True

Answer: b) True

Explanation:
Scrum is not a process, technique, or definitive method. It is a framework within which you can employ various processes and techniques.

20. What comprises Scrum? Select four possible answers.
a) Events
b) Reports
c) Burn-down Charts
d) Roles
e) Rules
f) Artifacts

Answer: a) Events, d) Roles, e) Rules, f) Artifacts

Explanation:
The Scrum framework consist of Scrum Teams and their associated roles, events, artifacts and rules. Each component within the framework serves a specific purpose and is essential to Scrum's success and usage. The rules of Scrum bind together the events, roles and artifacts, governing the relationships and interaction between them.

21. What are the three Scrum pillars?
a) Transparency
b) Inspection
c) Adaption
d) Agility
e) Self-organization
f) Cross-functionality

Answer: a) Transparency, b) Inspection, c) Adaption

Explanation:
Scrum is founded in empirical process control theory or empiricism. Empiricism asserts that knowledge comes form experience and making decisions based on what is known. Three pillars uphold every implementation of empirical process control: transparency, inspection and adaption.

3. Quiz Scrum Team

1. **What are the two essential features of a Scrum Team?**
a) It should have all competencies needed to accomplish the work without depending on others not part of the team
b) It should choose how best to accomplish their work, rather than being directed by others outside the team
c) It should use tools, processes and techniques approved by the organization
d) It should be flexible enough to complete all the work planned for the Sprint even if some team members are on vacation

Answer: a) It should have all competencies needed to accomplish the work without depending on others not part of the team, b) It should choose how best to accomplish their work, rather than being directed by others outside the team

Explanation:
Scrum Teams are self-organizing and cross-functional. Self-organizing teams choose how best to accomplish their work rather than being directed by others outside the team. Cross-functional teams have all competencies needed to accomplish the work without depending on others not part of the team.

2. Who builds the Scrum Team:
a) Product Owner
b) Development Team
c) Scrum Master
d) CEO
e) Key Stakeholder

Answer: a) Product Owner, b) Development Team, c) Scrum Master

Explanation:
The Scrum Team consists of a Product Owner, the Development Team and a Scrum Master.

3. Regarding the Daily Scrum the Scrum Master does the following (check all possible answers):
a) Ensures that the Development Team has the meeting
b) Is responsible for conducting the Daily Scrum
c) Teaches the Development Team to keep the Daily Scrum within the 15 minute time-box
d) If others are present at the Daily Scrum the Scrum Master ensures that they do not disrupt the meeting

Answer: a) Ensures that the Development Team has the meeting, c) Teaches the Development Team to keep the Daily Scrum within the 15-minute time-box, d) If others are present at the Daily Scrum the Scrum Master ensures that they do not disrupt the meeting

Explanation:
The Scrum Master
- ensures that the Development Team has the meeting but the Development Team is responsible for conducting the Daily Scrum
- teaches the Development Team to keep the Daily Scrum within the 15-minute time-box
- if others are present at the Daily Scrum the Scrum Master ensures that the do not disrupt the meeting

4. Select three characteristics of the Product Owner?
a) Lead facilitator of key stakeholder involvement
b) Product value maximizer
c) Lead Scrum evangelist in the organization
d) Facilitator of Scrum events
e) Product marketplace expert

Answer: a) Lead facilitator of key stakeholder involvement, b) Product value maximizer, e) Product marketplace expert

5. The team model in Scrum is designed to optimize which three main qualities?
a) Agility
b) Creativity
c) Flexibility
d) Productivity
e) Responsibility
f) Competence

Answer: b) Creativity, c) Flexibility, d) Productivity

Explanation:
The team model in Scrum is designed to optimize flexibility, creativity and productivity.

6. Who has the responsibility for the Product Backlog management?
a) Scrum Master
b) Development Team
c) Product Owner
d) Product Owner and Development Team
e) Key stakeholders

Answer: c) Product Owner

Explanation:
The Product Owner is the sole person responsible for managing the Product Backlog.

7. Who has to promote and support Scrum?
a) Scrum Master
b) Scrum Master and Product Owner
c) Product Owner
d) Development Team
e) Scrum Team

Answer: a) Scrum Master

Explanation:
The Scrum Master is responsible for promoting and supporting Scrum as defined in the Scrum Guide. Scrum Masters do this by helping everyone understand Scrum theory, practices, rules and values.

8. How does the Scrum Master help the Product Owner? Select three possible answers.

a) Understanding product planning in an empirical environment
b) Facilitating Scrum events as requested or needed
c) Finding techniques for effective Product Backlog management
d) Introducing cutting edge development practices
e) Leading and coaching the organization in the Scrum adoption

Answer: a) Understanding product planning in an empirical environment, b) Facilitating Scrum events as requested or needed, c) Finding techniques for effective Product Backlog management

Explanation:

The Scrum Master serves the Product Owner in several ways, including:

- ensuring that goals, scope and product domain are understood by everyone on the Scrum Team as well as possible
- finding techniques for effective Product Backlog management
- helping the Scrum Team understand the need for clear and concise Product Backlog items
- understanding product planning in an empirical environment
- ensuring the Product Owner knows how to arrange the Product Backlog to maximize value
- understanding and practicing agility
- facilitating Scrum events as requested or needed

9. What is included by Product Backlog management? Select three possible answers.

a) Moving Product Backlog items into the Sprint Backlog
b) Optimizing the value of the work the Development Team performs
c) Ensuring that the Product Backlog is visible, transparent and clear to all and shows what the Scrum Team will work on next
d) Presenting Product Backlog items to key stakeholders
e) Ordering the items in the Product Backlog to best achieve goals and missions

Answer: b) Optimizing the value of the work the Development Team performs, c) Ensuring that the Product Backlog is visible, transparent and clear to all and shows what the Scrum Team will work on next, e) Ordering the items in the Product Backlog to best achieve goals and missions

Explanation:
Product Backlog management includes:
- clearly expressing Product Backlog items
- ordering the items in the Product Backlog to best achieve goals and missions
- optimizing the value of the work the Development Team performs
- ensuring that the Product Backlog is visible, transparent and clear to all and shows what the Scrum Team will work on next
- ensuring the Development Team understands items in the Product Backlog to the level needed

10. Select three characteristics of the Development Team?

a) Scrum recognizes no titles for Development Team members other than Developer
b) Scrum recognizes no sub-teams in the Development Team
c) Having at least one test engineer in the Development Team
d) Accountability belongs to the Development Team as a whole
e) Having the Scrum Master as a part-time Developer in the Development Team

Answer: a) Scrum recognizes no titles for Development Team members other than Developer, b) Scrum recognizes no sub-teams in the Development Team, d) Accountability belongs to the Development Team as a whole

Explanation:
Development Teams have the following characteristics:
- they are self-organizing. No one (not even the Scrum Master) tells the Development Team how to turn Product Backlog into Increments of potentially releasable functionality
- Development Teams are cross-functional, with all of the skills as a team necessary to create a product Increment

- Scrum recognizes no titles for Development Team members other than Developer, regardless of the work being performed by the person. There are no exceptions to this rule
- Scrum recognizes no sub-teams in the Development Team, regardless of particular domains that need to be addressed like testing or business analysis. There are no exceptions to this rule
- individual Development Team members may have specialized skills and areas of focus but accountability belongs to the Development Team as a whole

11. If you are the Scrum Master and there are ten professionals (developers and testers) and the Product Owner. How do you distribute people between development teams? Choose all possible options:
a) 2 teams of 6 and 4 people (the professionals after a short meeting decided this is the best option)
b) 2 teams of 6 and 4 people (because it is good to have all the testers in a separate team)
c) 1 team of 10 people (because there is no reason to divide)
d) 3 teams of 4, 3 and 3 people (each team is cross-functional)

Answer: a) 2 teams of 6 and 4 people (the professionals after a short meeting decided this is the best option), d) 3 teams of 4, 3 and 3 people (each team is cross-functional)

Explanation:
Number of people in Development Team should be between 3 and 9. Each team should be cross-functional and self-organized.

Optimal Development Team size is small enough to remain nimble and large enough to complete significant work within a Sprint. Fewer than three Development Team members decrease interaction and results in smaller productivity gains. Having more than nine members requires too much coordination. The Product Owner and Scrum Master roles are not included in this count unless they are also executing the work of the Sprint Backlog.

12. How does the Scrum Master help the Development Team? Select three answers.

a) Coaching the Development Team in self-organization and cross-functionality
b) Removing impediments to the Development Team's progress
c) Helping the Development Team as the team leader
d) Helping the Development Team to create high-value products
e) Adding or removing developers from the Development Team in accordance with team velocity changes

Answer: a) Coaching the Development Team in self-organization and cross-functionality, b) Removing impediments to the Development Team's progress, d) Helping the Development Team to create high-value products

Explanation:
The Scrum Master serves the Development Team in several ways, including:
- coaching the Development Team in self-organization and cross-functionality
- helping the Development Team to create high-value products
- removing impediments to the Development Team's progress
- facilitating Scrum events as requested or needed

- coaching the Development Team in organizational environments in which Scrum is not yet fully adopted and understood

13. On big projects it is a good practice to have at least two Product.
a) True
b) False

Answer: b) False

Explanation:
The Product Owner is one persona, not a committee but the Product Owner may represent the desires of a committee in the Product Backlog.

14. Can Product Owner and Scrum Master also be a part of the Development Team?
a) No
b) Yes

Answer: b) Yes

Explanation:
Scrum does not prohibit the Product Owner or the Scrum Master do development work. However, it is not the best practice because it could create a conflict of interest.

15. How does the Scrum Master serve the organization? Select three answers.

a) Planning Scrum implementations within the organization
b) Mixing experienced developers and junior specialists across different Development Teams in the organization to speed up Scrum adoption
c) Leading and coaching the organization in the Scrum adoption
d) Making sure the key stakeholders are invited on all Scrum Reviews within organization
e) Working with other Scrum Masters to increase the effectiveness of the application of Scrum in the organization

Answer: a) Planning Scrum implementations within the organization, c) Leading and coaching the organization in the Scrum adoption, e) Working with other Scrum Masters to increase the effectiveness of the application of Scrum in the organization

Explanation:
The Scrum Master serves the organization in several ways, including:
- leading and coaching the organization in its Scrum adoption
- planning Scrum implementations within the organization
- helping employees and stakeholders understand and enact Scrum and empirical product development

- causing change that increases the productivity of the Scrum Team
- working with other Scrum Masters to increase the effectiveness of the application of Scrum in the organization

16. Usually the Scrum Master does not care about those outside the Scrum Team and is focussed primarily on the Scrum Team.
a) False
b) True

Answer: a) False

Explanation:
The Scrum Master is a servant-leader for the Scrum Team. The Scrum Master helps those outside the Scrum Team understand which of their interactions with the Scrum Team are helpful and which are not. The Scrum Master helps everyone change these interactions to maximize the value created by the Scrum Team.

4. Quiz Scrum Events

1. **Dependent on the size of the Development Team the Daily Scrum time-box can be changed.**
a) True
b) False

Answer: b) False

Explanation:
The Daily Scrum is a 15-minute time-boxed event for the Development Team of any size.

2. **In order to provide technical or domain advice other people than the Scrum Team can attend the Sprint Planning.**
a) False
b) True

Answer: b) True

Explanation:
The Development Team may also invite other people to attend in order to provide technical or domain advice.

3. **Put the following Scrum events in the right order.**
a) Sprint Review
b) Daily Scrum
c) Sprint Retrospective
d) Sprint Planning

Answer: d) Sprint Planning, b) Daily Scrum, a) Sprint Review, c) Sprint Retrospective

Explanation:
A Sprint begins with Sprint Planning followed by several Daily Scrum meetings, then there are Sprint Review and Sprint Retrospective.

4. **Who can participate in the Daily Scrum? Select all possible answers.**
a) Scrum Master
b) Development Team
c) Key stakeholders
d) Product Owner

Answer: b) Development Team

Explanation:
The Daily Scrum is an internal meeting for the Development Team. If others are present the Scrum Master ensures that they do not disrupt the meeting.

5. Please select a time-box for the following Scrum events: Sprint Review, Sprint Planning, Daily Scrum, Sprint Retrospective.

a) 3hours or less
b) 15 minutes
c) 8 hours or less
d) 4 hours or less

Answer: Sprint Review d) 4 hours or less, Sprint Planning c) 8 hours or less, Daily Scrum b) 15 minutes, Sprint Retrospective a) 3 hours or less

Explanation:
- Sprint Planning is time-boxed to a maximum of 8 hours for a one-month Sprint. For shorter Sprints the event is usually shorter
- The Daily Scrum is a 15-minute time-boxed event for the Development Team to synchronize activities and create a plan for the next 24 hours
- Sprint Review is a four-hour time-boxed meeting for one-month Sprints. For shorter Sprints the event is usually shorter
- Sprint Retrospective is a three-hour time-boxed meeting for one-month Sprints. For shorter Sprints the event is usually shorter

6. **The Daily Scrum should always take exactly 15 minutes. If your team managed doing it in 10 minutes, they should spend 5 more minutes on Product Backlog refinement, but no more.**
a) True
b) False

Answer: b) False

Explanation:
All events in Scrum are time-boxed. It means that every event has a maximum duration. However, the Scrum Guide does not require a minimal duration for any event. As Scrum Teams mature, they can do some events faster (e.g. Sprint Planning or Sprint Retrospective).

7. **Additional meetings that are not defined in Scrum are not allowed.**
a) False
b) True

Answer: a) False

Explanation:
Scrum allows additional meetings if they facilitate achieving the Sprint Goal.

8. **In the Sprint Planning. there is nothing to do for the Scrum Master. Only the Product Owner and the Development Team can participate.**
a) True
b) False

Answer: b) False

Explanation:
The work to be performed in the Sprint is planned at the Sprint Planning. This plan is created by the collaborative work of the entire Scrum Team.

9. **Select the two meetings in which people outside the Scrum Team are allowed to participate.**
a) Sprint Review
b) Daily Scrum
c) Sprint Planning
d) Sprint Retrospective

Answer: a) Sprint Review, c) Sprint Planning

Explanation:

- The Development Team may invite other people to attend the Sprint Planning in order to provide technical or domain advice
- The Product Owner is responsible for inviting the Key Stakeholders to the Sprint Review meeting

10. The structure of the Daily Scrum is predefined. Every team member should answer the three main questions:
- What did I do yesterday?
- What will I do today?
- Do I see any impediment

a) False
b) True

Answer: a) False

Explanation:
There is no any prescribed structure. The structure of the Daily Scrum is set by the Development Team and can be conducted in different ways if it focusses on progress toward the Sprint Goal. Some Development Teams will use questions, some will be more discussion based. It is still perfectly fine to use the questions but other ways of conducting the meeting are also possible.

11. Who crafts the Sprint Goal at the Sprint Planning?
a) Scrum Team
b) Product Owner
c) Scrum Master
d) Development Team
e) Key stakeholders

Answer: a) Scrum Team

Explanation:
After the Development Team forecasts the Product Backlog items it will deliver in the Sprint, the Scrum Team crafts a Sprint Goal.

12. What is the result of the Sprint Review?
a) Common understanding of progress toward the Sprint Goal and how progress is trending toward completing the work in the Sprint Backlog.
b) A revised Product Backlog that defines the probable Product Backlog items for the next Sprint
c) A list of improvements that the Scrum Team will implement in the next Sprint
d) Common understanding of what can be delivered in the increment and how will the work needed to deliver increment be achieved

Answer: b) A revised Product Backlog that defines the probable Product Backlog items for the next Sprint

Explanation:
The result of the Sprint Review is a revised Product Backlog that defines the probable Product Backlog items for the next Sprint. The Product Backlog may also be adjusted overall to meet new opportunities.

13. What are formal opportunities to inspect and adapt?
a) Daily Scrum
b) Sprint Planning
c) Sprint Retrospective
d) Sprint
e) Sprint Review

Answer: a) Daily Scrum, b) Sprint Planning, c) Sprint Retrospective, e) Sprint Review

Explanation:
Other than the Sprint itself, which is a container for all other events, each event in Scrum is a formal opportunity to inspect and adapt something. These events are specifically designed to enable critical transparency and inspection.

14. What is the time-box for a Sprint Planning?
a) Not more than 8 hours
b) As much as it is necessary to make task breakdown and estimations for all items in the Sprint Backlog
c) Not more than 4 hours
d) From 4 to 8 hours

Answer: a) Not more than 8 hours

Explanation:
Sprint Planning is time-boxed to a maximum of eight hours for a one-month Sprint.

15. What is the input to the Sprint Planning? Select four possible answers.
a) The latest product increment
b) Projected capacity of the Development Team during the Sprint
c) The Product Backlog
d) Past performance of the Development Team
e) Feedback from the key stakeholders
f) Feedback from the organization CEO

Answer: a) The latest product increment, b) Projected capacity of the Development Team during the Sprint, c) The Product Backlog, d) Past performance of the Development Team

Explanation:
The input to the Sprint Planning is the Product Backlog, the latest product Increment, projected capacity of the Development Team during the Sprint and past performance of the Development Team.

16. Who can cancel the Sprint?
a) Development Team
b) Scrum Master
c) Product Owner
d) Key stakeholders
e) Product Owner and Scrum Master

Answer: c) Product Owner

Explanation:
Only the Product Owner has the authority to cancel the Sprint, although he or she may do so under influence from the stakeholders, the Development Team or the Scrum Master.

17. "Definition of Done" can be adapted in each Sprint Retrospective.

a) False
b) True

Answer: b) True

Explanation:
During each Sprint Retrospective, the Scrum Team plans ways to increase product quality by improving work processes or adapting the definition of "Done", if appropriate and not in conflict with product or organizational standards.

18. What happens during the Sprint? Select three answers.

a) Quality goals do not decrease
b) No changes are made that would endanger the Sprint Goal
c) Sprint scope is defined at the Sprint Planning and cannot be changed
d) Scope may be clarified and re-negotiated between the Product Owner and Development Team as more is learned
e) The Sprint Goal is changed frequently to reflect the status of the remaining work

Answer: a) Quality goals do not decrease, b) No changes are made that would endanger the Sprint Goal, d) Scope may be clarified and re-negotiated between the Product Owner and Development Team as more is learned

Explanation:
During the Sprint:
- no changes are made that would endanger the Sprint Goal
- quality goals do not decrease
- scope may be clarified and re-negotiated between the Product Owner and the Development Team as more is learned

19. What happens when a Sprint is cancelled? Select three answers.

a) All incomplete Product Backlog items are re-estimated and put back on the Product Backlog
b) If part of the work is potentially releasable the Product Owner typically accepts it
c) Any completed and "Done" Product Backlog items are reviewed
d) Several top Product Backlog items are taken into the Sprint Backlog to replace the obsolete items
e) At the Sprint Retrospective the Scrum Master determines who from the Development Team is responsible for cancelling the Sprint

Answer: a) All incomplete Product Backlog items are re-estimated and put back on the Product Backlog, b) If part of the work is potentially releasable the Product Owner typically accepts it, c) Any completed and "Done" Product Backlog items are reviewed

Explanation:
When a Sprint is cancelled any completed and "Done" Product Backlog items are reviewed. If part of the work is potentially releasable the Product Owner typically accepts it. All incomplete Product Backlog items are re-estimated and put back on the Product Backlog.

20. What are the three questions, provided by the Scrum Guide, that can be used at the Daily Scrum?

a) Do I see any impediment that prevents me or the Development Team from meeting the Sprint Goal?
b) What did I do yesterday that helped the Development Team meet the Sprint Goal?
c) Do I have complete understanding of the Sprint Backlog item I am working on?
d) What will I do today to help the Development Team meet the Sprint Goal?
e) Did I explain all the discovered issues I found yesterday to the Product Owner?

Answer: a) Do I see any impediment that prevents me or the Development Team from meeting the Sprint Goal?, b) What did I do yesterday that helped the Development Team meet the Sprint Goal?, d) What will I do today to help the Development Team meet the Sprint Goal?

Explanation:
The structure of the Daily Scrum is set by the Development Team and can be conducted in different ways if it focuses on progress toward the Sprint Goal. Some Development Teams will use questions, some will be more discussion based. Her is an example of what might be used:
- What did I do yesterday that helped the Development Team meet the Sprint Goal?

- What will I do today to help the Development Team meet the Sprint Goal?
- Do I see any impediment that prevents me or the Development Team from meeting the Sprint Goal?

21. What provides guidance to the Development Team on why it is building the Increment?
a) Product Owner
b) Sprint Backlog
c) Scrum Master
d) Sprint Goal

Answer: d) Sprint Goal

Explanation:
The Sprint Goal is an objective set for the Sprint that can be met through the implementation of Product Backlog. It provides guidance to the Development Team on why it is building the Increment.

22. It is allowed to skip the Daily Scrum if there is nothing to talk about.
a) Yes
b) No

Answer: b) No

Explanation:
Each event in Scrum is a formal opportunity to inspect and adapt something. These events are specifically designed to enable critical transparency and inspection. Failure to include any of these events results in reduced transparency and is lost opportunity to inspect and adapt.

23. In which meetings the key stakeholders are allowed to participate? Select all appropriate answers.

a) Sprint Planning
b) Sprint Review
c) Daily Scrum
d) Sprint Retrospective

Answer: b) Sprint Review

Explanation:
The Key Stakeholders are allowed to participate only in the Sprint Review meeting. However, any member of the Scrum Team can interact with them any time.

24. Which questions are answered in the Sprint Planning? Select two answers.
a) Who will be responsible for each item in the Sprint Backlog?
b) What ca be delivered in the Increment resulting from the upcoming Sprint?
c) How will the work needed to deliver the Increment be achieved?
d) What new technologies could be used to speed up the Development Team velocity?
e) What is the size of the Technical Debt and how it could be removed?

Answer: b) What ca be delivered in the Increment resulting from the upcoming Sprint?, c) How will the work needed to deliver the Increment be achieved

Explanation:
Sprint Planning answers the following:
- What can be delivered in the Increment resulting from the upcoming Sprint?
- How will the work needed to deliver the Increment be achieved?

25. **Who participates in the Sprint Planning? Select three answers.**
a) Scrum Master
b) Product Owner
c) Development Team
d) Team Manager
e) Key stakeholders

Answer: a) Scrum Master, b) Product Owner, c) Development Team

Explanation:
The work to be performed in the Sprint is planned at the Sprint Planning. This plan is created by the collaborative work of the entire Scrum Team

26. **The Development Team should be able to explain to the Product Owner and Scrum Master how it wants to work as a self-organizing team to reach the Sprint Goal and create the anticipated Increment.**
a) False
b) True

Answer: b) True

Explanation:
By the end of the Sprint Planning, the Development Team should be able to explain to the Product Owner and Scrum Master how it intends to work as a self-organizing team to accomplish the Sprint Goal and create the anticipated Increment.

27. If only work planned for the first days of the Sprint is decomposed to units of one day or less, could the Sprint Planning be finished?

a) No, all items in the Sprint Backlog should be decomposed to units of one day or less by the end of the Sprint Planning
b) Yes, if the remaining work is also estimated, maybe in bigger units

Answer: b) Yes, if the remaining work is also estimated, maybe in bigger units

Explanation:
The Scrum Guide requires only the work planned for the first days of the Sprint is decomposed by the end of the Sprint Planning, often to units of one day or less. However, the Development Team should be able to explain to the Product Owner and Scrum Master how it intends to work as a self-organizing team to accomplish the Sprint Goal and create the anticipated Increment.

28. What is the purpose of the Sprint Retrospective? Select three answers.
a) Identify and order the major items that went well and potential improvements
b) Create a plan for implementing improvements to the way the Scrum Team does its work
c) Get feedback from the key stakeholders invited by the Product Owner
d) Inspect how the last Sprint went with regards to people, relationships, process and tools
e) Get technical or domain advice from specialists invited by the Development Team or the Scrum Master

Answer: a) Identify and order the major items that went well and potential improvements, b) Create a plan for implementing improvements to the way the Scrum Team does its work, d) Inspect how the last Sprint went with regards to people, relationships, process and tools

Explanation:
The purpose of the Sprint Retrospective is to:
- inspect how the last Sprint went with regards to people, relationships, process and tools
- identify and order the major items that went well and potential improvements
Create a plan for implementing improvements to the way the Scrum Team does its work

29. Who participates in the Sprint Review? Select all possible answers.
a) Development Team
b) Scrum Master
c) Key stakeholders
d) Product Owner
e) Organization CEO

Answer: a) Development Team, b) Scrum Master, c) Key stakeholders, d) Product Owner

Explanation:
During the Sprint Review, the Scrum Team and stakeholders collaborate about what was done in the Sprint. Based on that and any changes to the Product Backlog during the Sprint, attendees collaborate on the next things that could be done to optimize value.

30. What is the Sprint Retrospective?
a) It is a meeting to inspect the increment and adapt the Product Backlog if needed
b) It is the key inspect and adapt meeting
c) It is a meeting where the Development Team synchronizes activities and creates a plan for the next 24 hours
d) It is an opportunity for the Scrum Team to inspect itself and create a plan for improvements to be enacted during the next Sprint

Answer: d) It is an opportunity for the Scrum Team to inspect itself and create a plan for improvements to be enacted during the next Sprint

Explanation:
The Sprint Retrospective is an opportunity for the Scrum Team to inspect itself and create a plan for improvements to be enacted during the next Sprint.

5. Quiz Scrum Artifacts

1. **Who is responsible for coping with incomplete transparency?**
a) Scrum Master
b) Product Owner
c) Development Team
d) Scrum Team

Answer: a) Scrum Master

Explanation:
The Scrum Master's job is to work with the Scrum Team and the organization to increase the transparency of the artifacts. This work usually involves learning, convincing and change.

2. **Who has the responsibility for the Product Backlog?**
a) Scrum Master
b) Product Owner
c) Product Owner and Scrum Master
d) Scrum Master and Development Team
e) Product Owner and Development Team
f) Development Team

Answer: b) Product Owner

Explanation:
The Product Owner is responsible for the Product Backlog including its content, availability and ordering.

3. How does "Definition of Done" help to the Scrum Team? Select three possible answers.

a) Definition of Done guides the Development Team in knowing how many Product Backlog items it can select during a Sprint Planning
b) Definition of Done ensures artifact transparency
c) Definition of Done helps in inspection and adaption
d) Definition of Done is used to assess when work is complete on the product increment
e) Definition of Done helps to calculate velocity of the Scrum Team

Answer: a) Definition of Done guides the Development Team in knowing how many Product Backlog items it can select during a Sprint Planning, b) Definition of Done ensures artifact transparency, d) Definition of Done is used to assess when work is complete on the product increment

Explanation:
Definition of Done:
- is used to assess when work is complete on the product Increment
- guides the Development Team in knowing how many Product Backlog items it can select during a Sprint Planning
- ensures artifact transparency

4. At the Sprint Retrospective meeting the Scrum Team identified some improvements that can be done. What should the Scrum Team do? Select the best answer.
a) Make sure the Sprint Backlog for the next Sprint includes at least one high priority process improvement.
b) Assign a responsible team member for at least one improvement. Check the progress at the next Sprint Retrospective.
c) Make sure the Sprint Backlog for the next Sprint includes all the improvements.
d) Assign responsible team members for every improvement. Check the progress at the next Sprint Retrospective.

Answer: a) Make sure the Sprint Backlog for the next Sprint includes at least one high priority process improvement.

Explanation:
The Sprint Backlog makes visible all the work that the Development Team identifies as necessary to meet the Sprint Goal. To ensure continuous improvement it includes at least one high priority process improvement identified in the previous Retrospective meeting.

5. What are three Product Backlog features?

a) As long as a product exists, its Product Backlog also exists
b) It is dynamic
c) It is never complete
d) A Product Backlog could be closed when it contains no items to include into the next Sprint
e) When the final version of a product is rolled out, its Product Backlog is dismissed

Answer: a) As long as a product exists, its Product Backlog also exists, b) It is dynamic, c) It is never complete

Explanation:
A Product Backlog is never complete. The earliest development of it only lays out the initially known and best understood requirements. The Product Backlog evolves as the product and the environment in which it will be used evolves. The Product Backlog is dynamic, it constantly changes to identify what the product needs to be appropriate, competitive and useful. As long as a product exists its Product Backlog also exists.

6. **The same Product Backlog should be used by all Development Teams working on the same product.**
a) True
b) False

Answer: a) True

Explanation:
Multiple Scrum Teams often work together on the same product. One Product Backlog is used to describe the upcoming work on the product.

7. **Who has the responsibility for all estimates in the Product Backlog?**
a) Scrum Master
b) Product Owner
c) Scrum Team
d) Development Team
e) Scrum Master and Development Team
f) Product Owner and Scrum Master
g) Product Owner and Development Team

Answer: d) Development Team
Explanation:
The Development Team is responsible for all estimates in the Product Backlog. The Product Owner may influence the Development Team by helping it understand and select trade-offs but the people who will perform the work make the final estimate.

8. **Who can make changes in the Product Backlog?**
a) The Development Team but with permission of the Product Owner
b) The Product Owner
c) Anyone
d) The key stakeholders

Answer: a) The Development Team but with permission of the Product Owner, b) The Product Owner

Explanation:
The Product Owner is the sole person responsible for the Product Backlog. However, he or she can delegate some work related to Product Backlog management to the Development Team.

9. What is the Sprint Backlog?
a) The Product Backlog items selected for this Sprint plus a set of Development Team internal tasks
b) The Product Backlog items selected for this Sprint
c) The Product Backlog items selected for this Sprint plus the plan for delivering them

Answer: c) The Product Backlog items selected for this Sprint plus the plan for delivering them

Explanation:
The Sprint Backlog is the set of Product Backlog items selected for the Sprint plus a plan for delivering the product Increment and realizing the Sprint Goal.

10. What is the order of tasks in the Product Backlog?
a) The recently added items at the top
b) Alphabetical
c) Less valuable and most unclear items at the bottom
d) The less clear items at the top

Answer: c) Less valuable and most unclear items at the bottom

Explanation:
The Product Owner is responsible for placing the most valuable and clear items at the top of the Product Backlog.

11. What is the Increment?
a) All items in the Sprint Backlog that could be released regardless of whether the Product Owner decides to actually do it
b) The sum of all the Product Backlog items completed during the Sprint
c) The sum of all the Product Backlog items completed during the Sprint and the value of the increments of all previous Sprints
d) All "done" items in the Sprint Backlog

Answer: c) The sum of all the Product Backlog items completed during the Sprint and the value of the increments of all previous Sprints

Explanation:
The Increment is the sum of all the Product Backlog items completed during the Sprint and the value of the increments of all previous Sprints.

12. The Sprint Backlog is created at the Sprint Planning. The Development Team is prohibited to add new work into the Sprint Backlog later.
a) True
b) False

Answer: b) False

Explanation:
The Development Team modifies the Sprint Backlog throughout the Sprint and the Sprint Backlog emerges during the Sprint. This emergence occurs as the Development Team works through the plan and learns more about the work needed to achieve the Sprint Goal. As new work is required the Development Team adds it to the Sprint Backlog.

13. Who can change the Sprint Backlog during the Sprint?
a) Development Team
b) Product Owner
c) Scrum Team
d) Scrum Master
e) Development Team and Product Owner

Answer: a) Development Team

Explanation:
Only the Development Team can change its Sprint Backlog during a Sprint. The Sprint Backlog is a highly visible, real-time picture of the work that the Development Team plans to accomplish during the Sprint and it belongs solely to the Development Team.

14. What belongs solely to the Development Team?
a) Product Backlog
b) Sprint Backlog
c) "Definition of Done"
d) Increment

Answer: b) Sprint Backlog

Explanation:
Only the Development Team can change its Sprint Backlog during a Sprint. The Sprint Backlog is a highly visible, real-time picture of the work that the Development Team plans to accomplish during the Sprint and it belongs solely to the Development Team.

15. Who is responsible for tracking the total work remaining in the Sprint Backlog to project the likelihood of achieving the Sprint Goal?
a) Scrum Master
b) Scrum Team
c) Development Team
d) Product Owner
e) Product Owner and Development Team

Answer: c) Development Team

Explanation:
At any point in time in a Sprint the total work remaining in the Sprint Backlog can be summed. The Development Team tracks this total work remaining at least for every Daily Scrum to project the likelihood of achieving the Sprint Goal. By tracking the remaining work throughout the Sprint the Development Team can manage its progress.

16. What are the Scrum Artifacts? Select all possible answers.

a) Increment
b) Sprint Backlog
c) Product Backlog
d) Sprint Goal
e) The list of removed impediments

Answer: a) Increment, b) Sprint Backlog, c) Product Backlog

Explanation:
The Scrum artifacts are Product Backlog, sprint Backlog and Increment.

17. **How many percent of the capacity of the Development Team does Product Backlog refinement usually take?**
a) Not more than 5%
b) The Development Team is not authorized for Product Backlog refinement
c) Not more than 10%
d) Not more than 20%

Answer: c) Not more than 10%

Explanation:
Product Backlog refinement usually consumes no more than 10% of the capacity of the Development Team.

18. **Who has the responsibility for the monitoring of the remaining work towards the project goal?**
a) Product Owner and Development Team
b) Product Owner
c) Scrum Master and Development Team
d) Scrum Master
e) Scrum Team
f) Development Team

Answer: b) Product Owner

Explanation:
The Product Owner tracks total remaining at least every Sprint Review. The Product Owner compares this amount with work remaining at previous Sprint Revies to assess progress toward completing projected work by the desired time for the goal. This information is made transparent to all stakeholders.

19. Who creates the Increment?
a) Development Team
b) Scrum Team
c) Product Owner
d) Scrum Master
e) Development Team and Product Owner

Answer: a) Development Team

Explanation:
Only members of the Development Team create the Increment.

20. What could be a source of requirements for any changes to be made to the product?
a) Key stakeholders
b) CEO of the organization
c) Product Backlog

Answer: c) Product Backlog

Explanation:
The Product Backlog is an ordered list of everything that might be needed in the product and is the single source of requirements for any changes to be mode to the product.

6. Exam Preparation PSM

6.1. Exam Preparation

First of all, please read the Scrum Guide. Then read the Scrum Guide and afterwards please read the Scrum Guide again and again...until you understood every single topic. Next to the Scrum Guide you have several other possibilities for a good Scrum Knowledge, e.g. the Scrum.org community forum.

After that you can also prepare with some "Open Assessments" via Scrum.org but please keep in mind that you have much more time for those questions and to my opinion they are very easy and do not represent the level of the certification exam. Please also pass those "Open Assessments" several times until you reach 100% every time in just a couple of minutes.

Following this, you can start with the sample exam and also repeat it several times. Afterwards you should have a good knowledge of Scrum.

Congratulations, you are ready for the real certification exam!

6.2. Exam Process

Before you can start with your exam you have to buy a password via Scrum.org. Actually, you have to pay 150 USD for it. The password has no expiration date but you can use it for only one try.

If you type in your password and start the certification exam the countdown of 60 minutes begins to run. Within this time, you have to answer 80 questions and 85% have to be correct. If you want to you can postpone difficult questions and answer them later.

6.3. Sample Exam Questions

1. **Who creates the 'Definition of Done'?**
a) Scrum Master
b) Product Owner
c) Scrum Team
d) Development Team

2. **What are the two essential features of a Scrum Team?**
a) It should have all competencies needed to accomplish the work without depending on others not part of the team
b) It should choose how best to accomplish their work, rather than being directed by others outside the team
c) It should use tools, processes and techniques approved by the organization
d) It should be flexible enough to complete all the work planned for the Sprint even if some team members are on vacation
3. **Dependent on the size of the Development Team the Daily Scrum time-box can be changed.**
a) True
b) False

4. **Who is responsible for coping with incomplete transparency?**
a) Scrum Master
b) Product Owner
c) Development Team
d) Scrum Team

5. **Select the five Scrum values.**
a) Openness
b) Courage
c) Commitment
d) Self-organization
e) Focus
f) Respect
g) Effectiveness
h) Agility

6. **Who builds the Scrum Team:**
a) Product Owner
b) Development Team
c) Scrum Master
d) CEO
e) Key Stakeholder

7. In order to provide technical or domain advice other people than the Scrum Team can attend the Sprint Planning.
a) False
b) True

8. Who has the responsibility for the Product Backlog?
a) Scrum Master
b) Product Owner
c) Product Owner and Scrum Master
d) Scrum Master and Development Team
e) Product Owner and Development Team
f) Development Team

9. What is shown by the 'Cone of Uncertainty'?
a) How much work remains till the end of the Sprint
b) How much is known about the product over time
c) Hierarchy of tasks that comprise a project
d) Dependencies, start times and stop times for project tasks

10. Regarding the Daily Scrum the Scrum Master does the following (check all possible answers):
a) Ensures that the Development Team has the meeting
b) Is responsible for conducting the Daily Scrum
c) Teaches the Development Team to keep the Daily Scrum within the 15-minute time-box
d) If others are present at the Daily Scrum the Scrum Master ensures that they do not disrupt the meeting

11. Put the following Scrum events in the right order.
a) Sprint Review
b) Daily Scrum
c) Sprint Retrospective
d) Sprint Planning

12. How does "Definition of Done" help to the Scrum Team? Select three possible answers.

a) Definition of Done guides the Development Team in knowing how many Product Backlog items it can select during a Sprint Planning
b) Definition of Done ensures artifact transparency
c) Definition of Done helps in inspection and adaption
d) Definition of Done is used to assess when work is complete on the product increment
e) Definition of Done helps to calculate velocity of the Scrum Team

13. Scrum is founded on:
a) Kanban system
b) Empirical criticism
c) Empiricism
d) Common sense

14. Select three characteristics of the Product Owner?
a) Lead facilitator of key stakeholder involvement
b) Product value maximizer
c) Lead Scrum evangelist in the organization
d) Facilitator of Scrum events
e) Product marketplace expert

15. Who can participate in the Daily Scrum? Select all possible answers.
a) Scrum Master
b) Development Team
c) Key stakeholders
d) Product Owner

16. At the Sprint Retrospective meeting the Scrum Team identified some improvements that can be done. What should the Scrum Team do? Select the best answer.
a) Make sure the Sprint Backlog for the next Sprint includes at least one high priority process improvement.
b) Assign a responsible team member for at least one improvement. Check the progress at the next Sprint Retrospective.
c) Make sure the Sprint Backlog for the next Sprint includes all the improvements.
d) Assign responsible team members for every improvement. Check the progress at the next Sprint Retrospective.

17. Where do we use Scrum? Check all possible answers.
a) Development and sustaining of cloud and other operational environments
b) Managing the operation of an organization
c) Research and identifying of viable markets, technologies and product capabilities
d) Development of products and enhancements
e) Development of almost everything we use in our daily live as individuals and societies
f) Development of software and hardware

18. The team model in Scrum is designed to optimize which three main qualities?
a) Agility
b) Creativity
c) Flexibility
d) Productivity
e) Responsibility
f) Competence

19. **Please select a time-box for the following Scrum events: Sprint Review, Sprint Planning, Daily Scrum, Sprint Retrospective.**
a) 3hours or less
b) 15 minutes
c) 8 hours or less
d) 4 hours or less

20. **What are three Product Backlog features?**
a) As long as a product exists, its Product Backlog also exists
b) It is dynamic
c) It is never complete
d) A Product Backlog could be closed when it contains no items to include into the next Sprint
e) When the final version of a product is rolled out, its Product Backlog is dismissed

21. **What is shown by the 'Burn-down Chart'?**
a) How much work remains till the end of the Sprint
b) Dependencies, start times and stop times for project tasks
c) The evolution of the amount of uncertainty during a project
d) Hierarchy of tasks that comprise a project

22. Who has the responsibility for the Product Backlog management?
a) Scrum Master
b) Development Team
c) Product Owner
d) Product Owner and Development Team
e) Key stakeholders

23. The Daily Scrum should always take exactly 15 minutes. If your team managed doing it in 10 minutes, they should spend 5 more minutes on Product Backlog refinement, but no more.
a) True
b) False

24. The same Product Backlog should be used by all Development Teams working on the same product.
a) True
b) False

25. What is the meaning of the word 'development' in the context of Scrum? Select the best answer.
a) Development of an operational environment for the product
b) Product development, its releasing and sustaining
c) Software and hardware development
d) Research and identifying of viable market, technologies and product capabilities
e) Complex work that can include all the suggested options and even more

26. Who has to promote and support Scrum?
a) Scrum Master
b) Scrum Master and Product Owner
c) Product Owner
d) Development Team
e) Scrum Team

27. Additional meetings that are not defined in Scrum are not allowed.
a) False
b) True

28. Who has the responsibility for all estimates in the Product Backlog?
a) Scrum Master
b) Product Owner
c) Scrum Team
d) Development Team
e) Scrum Master and Development Team
f) Product Owner and Scrum Master
g) Product Owner and Development Team

29. What is the essence of Scrum? Select the best answer.
a) A small team of people that is highly flexible and adaptive
b) The Scrum Guide
c) The Development Team
d) The Scrum Master and the Product Owner

30. **How does the Scrum Master help the Product Owner? Select three possible answers.**
a) Understanding product planning in an empirical environment
b) Facilitating Scrum events as requested or needed
c) Finding techniques for effective Product Backlog management
d) Introducing cutting edge development practices
e) Leading and coaching the organization in the Scrum adoption

31. **In the Sprint Planning. there is nothing to do for the Scrum Master. Only the Product Owner and the Development Team can participate.**
a) True
b) False

32. **Who can make changes in the Product Backlog?**
a) The Development Team but with permission of the Product Owner
b) The Product Owner
c) Anyone
d) The key stakeholders

33. 'Definition of Done' is created in the first Sprint and cannot be changed until the final product release.
a) True
b) False

34. What is included by Product Backlog management? Select three possible answers.
a) Moving Product Backlog items into the Sprint Backlog
b) Optimizing the value of the work the Development Team performs
c) Ensuring that the Product Backlog is visible, transparent and clear to all and shows what the Scrum Team will work on next
d) Presenting Product Backlog items to key stakeholders
e) Ordering the items in the Product Backlog to best achieve goals and missions

35. Select the two meetings in which people outside the Scrum Team are allowed to participate.
a) Sprint Review
b) Daily Scrum
c) Sprint Planning
d) Sprint Retrospective

36. What is the Sprint Backlog?
a) The Product Backlog items selected for this Sprint plus a set of Development Team internal tasks
b) The Product Backlog items selected for this Sprint
c) The Product Backlog items selected for this Sprint plus the plan for delivering them

37. It is a good practice to sometimes have a special technical Sprint that consists only of tasks removing the technical debt without implementing any new functionality.
a) True
b) False

38. Select three characteristics of the Development Team?
a) Scrum recognizes no titles for Development Team members other than Developer
b) Scrum recognizes no sub-teams in the Development Team
c) Having at least one test engineer in the Development Team
d) Accountability belongs to the Development Team as a whole
e) Having the Scrum Master as a part-time Developer in the Development Team

39. The structure of the Daily Scrum is predefined. Every team member should answer the three main questions:
 - What did I do yesterday?
 - What will I do today?
 - Do I see any impediment

a) False
b) True

40. What is the Sprint Backlog?
a) The Product Backlog items selected for this Sprint plus a set of Development Team internal tasks
b) The Product Backlog items selected for this Sprint
c) The Product Backlog items selected for this Sprint plus the plan for delivering them

41. How often should Scrum users inspect Scrum artifacts and progress towards a Sprint Goal?
a) Frequently, but it should not get in the way of the work
b) As frequently as possible
c) After the Daily Scrum
d) At the Sprint Review

42. If you are the Scrum Master and there are ten professionals (developers and testers) and the Product Owner. How do you distribute people between development teams? Choose all possible options:
a) 2 teams of 6 and 4 people (the professionals after a short meeting decided this is the best option)
b) 2 teams of 6 and 4 people (because it is good to have all the testers in a separate team)
c) 1 team of 10 people (because there is no reason to divide)
d) 3 teams of 4, 3 and 3 people (each team is cross-functional)

43. Who crafts the Sprint Goal at the Sprint Planning?
a) Scrum Team
b) Product Owner
c) Scrum Master
d) Development Team
e) Key stakeholders

44. What is the order of tasks in the Product Backlog?
a) The recently added items at the top
b) Alphabetical
c) Less valuable and most unclear items at the bottom
d) The less clear items at the top

45. Is it normal to have a 'hardening' Sprint to remove technical debts and prepare the product for the next release.
a) True
b) False

46. How does the Scrum Master help the Development Team? Select three answers.
a) Coaching the Development Team in self-organization and cross-functionality
b) Removing impediments to the Development Team's progress
c) Helping the Development Team as the team leader
d) Helping the Development Team to create high-value products
e) Adding or removing developers from the Development Team in accordance with team velocity changes

47. What is the result of the Sprint Review?
a) Common understanding of progress toward the Sprint Goal and how progress is trending toward completing the work in the Sprint Backlog.
b) A revised Product Backlog that defines the probable Product Backlog items for the next Sprint
c) A list of improvements that the Scrum Team will implement in the next Sprint
d) Common understanding of what can be delivered in the increment and how will the work needed to deliver increment be achieved

48. What are formal opportunities to inspect and adapt?
a) Daily Scrum
b) Sprint Planning
c) Sprint Retrospective
d) Sprint
e) Sprint Review

49. What is the Increment?
a) All items in the Sprint Backlog that could be released regardless of whether the Product Owner decides to actually do it
b) The sum of all the Product Backlog items completed during the Sprint
c) The sum of all the Product Backlog items completed during the Sprint and the value of the increments of all previous Sprints
d) All "done" items in the Sprint Backlog

50. All the Scrum Teams working on the same product should have the same Sprint duration.
a) False
b) True

51. On big projects it is a good practice to have at least two Product.
a) True
b) False

52. What is the time-box for a Sprint Planning?
a) Not more than 8 hours
b) As much as it is necessary to make task breakdown and estimations for all items in the Sprint Backlog
c) Not more than 4 hours
d) From 4 to 8 hours

53. What is the input to the Sprint Planning? Select four possible answers.
a) The latest product increment
b) Projected capacity of the Development Team during the Sprint
c) The Product Backlog
d) Past performance of the Development Team
e) Feedback from the key stakeholders
f) Feedback from the organization CEO

54. The Sprint Backlog is created at the Sprint Planning. The Development Team is prohibited to add new work into the Sprint Backlog later.
a) True
b) False

55. **What should be taken into account for the 'Definition of Done'? Check two possible answers.**
a) Definition of Done of other Scrum Teams working on the same product
b) Conventions, standards and guidelines of the organization
c) Experience of the Product Owner
d) Definition of Done of other Scrum Teams working on other products
e) Advice of the Scrum Master

56. **Can Product Owner and Scrum Master also be a part of the Development Team?**
a) No
b) Yes

57. **Who can cancel the Sprint?**
a) Development Team
b) Scrum Master
c) Product Owner
d) Key stakeholders
e) Product Owner and Scrum Master

58. "Definition of Done" can be adapted in each Sprint Retrospective.
a) False
b) True

59. Who can change the Sprint Backlog during the Sprint?
a) Development Team
b) Product Owner
c) Scrum Team
d) Scrum Master
e) Development Team and Product Owner

60. The Sprint is cancelled if an item in the Sprint Backlog cannot be finished by the end of the Sprint.
a) True
b) False

61. How does the Scrum Master serve the organization? Select three answers.
a) Planning Scrum implementations within the organization
b) Mixing experienced developers and junior specialists across different Development Teams in the organization to speed up Scrum adoption
c) Leading and coaching the organization in the Scrum adoption
d) Making sure the key stakeholders are invited on all Scrum Reviews within organization
e) Working with other Scrum Masters to increase the effectiveness of the application of Scrum in the organization

62. What happens during the Sprint? Select three answers.
a) Quality goals do not decrease
b) No changes are made that would endanger the Sprint Goal
c) Sprint scope is defined at the Sprint Planning and cannot be changed
d) Scope may be clarified and re-negotiated between the Product Owner and Development Team as more is learned
e) The Sprint Goal is changed frequently to reflect the status of the remaining work

63. What happens when a Sprint is cancelled? Select three answers.

a) All incomplete Product Backlog items are re-estimated and put back on the Product Backlog
b) If part of the work is potentially releasable the Product Owner typically accepts it
c) Any completed and "Done" Product Backlog items are reviewed
d) Several top Product Backlog items are taken into the Sprint Backlog to replace the obsolete items
e) At the Sprint Retrospective the Scrum Master determines who from the Development Team is responsible for cancelling the Sprint

64. What are the three questions, provided by the Scrum Guide, that can be used at the Daily Scrum?

a) Do I see any impediment that prevents me or the Development Team from meeting the Sprint Goal?
b) What did I do yesterday that helped the Development Team meet the Sprint Goal?
c) Do I have complete understanding of the Sprint Backlog item I am working on?
d) What will I do today to help the Development Team meet the Sprint Goal?
e) Did I explain all the discovered issues I found yesterday to the Product Owner?

65. What belongs solely to the Development Team?
a) Product Backlog
b) Sprint Backlog
c) "Definition of Done"
d) Increment

66. In Scrum only those Scrum components and rules which fit most for a particular project should be used.
a) False
b) True

67. Usually the Scrum Master does not care about those outside the Scrum Team and is focussed primarily on the Scrum Team.
a) False
b) True

68. What provides guidance to the Development Team on why it is building the Increment?
a) Product Owner
b) Sprint Backlog
c) Scrum Master
d) Sprint Goal

69. It is allowed to skip the Daily Scrum if there is nothing to talk about.
a) Yes
b) No

70. In which meetings the key stakeholders are allowed to participate? Select all appropriate answers.
a) Sprint Planning
b) Sprint Review
c) Daily Scrum
d) Sprint Retrospective

71. Who is responsible for tracking the total work remaining in the Sprint Backlog to project the likelihood of achieving the Sprint Goal?
a) Scrum Master
b) Scrum Team
c) Development Team
d) Product Owner
e) Product Owner and Development Team

72. What is Scrum?
a) A framework within which people can address complex adaptive problems, while delivering valuable products.
b) A software development methodology which is intended to improve software quality.
c) A sequential design process, uses in software development process, in which progress is seen as flowing steadily downwards.

73. Which questions are answered in the Sprint Planning? Select two answers.
a) Who will be responsible for each item in the Sprint Backlog?
b) What ca be delivered in the Increment resulting from the upcoming Sprint?
c) How will the work needed to deliver the Increment be achieved?
d) What new technologies could be used to speed up the Development Team velocity?
e) What is the size of the Technical Debt and how it could be removed?

74. What are the Scrum Artifacts? Select all possible answers.
a) Increment
b) Sprint Backlog
c) Product Backlog
d) Sprint Goal
e) The list of removed impediments

75. When must an adjustment be made ff an inspector determines that one or more aspects of a process deviate outside acceptable limits?
a) As soon as possible to minimize further deviation
b) After clarifying all the details with the Product Owner
c) The deviations should be discussed at the Daily Scrum and then an adjustment must be made
d) After Scrum Master approval

76. Who participates in the Sprint Planning? Select three answers.
a) Scrum Master
b) Product Owner
c) Development Team
d) Team Manager
e) Key stakeholders

77. How many percent of the capacity of the Development Team does Product Backlog refinement usually take?
a) Not more than 5%
b) The Development Team is not authorized for Product Backlog refinement
c) Not more than 10%
d) Not more than 20%

78. Scrum is neither a process nor technique. True or false?
a) False
b) True

79. The Development Team should be able to explain to the Product Owner and Scrum Master how it wants to work as a self-organizing team to reach the Sprint Goal and create the anticipated Increment.
a) False
b) True

80. Who has the responsibility for the monitoring of the remaining work towards the project goal?
a) Product Owner and Development Team
b) Product Owner
c) Scrum Master and Development Team
d) Scrum Master
e) Scrum Team
f) Development Team

81. What comprises Scrum? Select four possible answers.
a) Events
b) Reports
c) Burn-down Charts
d) Roles
e) Rules
f) Artifacts

82. If only work planned for the first days of the Sprint is decomposed to units of one day or less, could the Sprint Planning be finished?
a) No, all items in the Sprint Backlog should be decomposed to units of one day or less by the end of the Sprint Planning
b) Yes, if the remaining work is also estimated, maybe in bigger units

83. Who creates the Increment?
a) Development Team
b) Scrum Team
c) Product Owner
d) Scrum Master
e) Development Team and Product Owner

84. What are the three Scrum pillars?
a) Transparency
b) Inspection
c) Adaption
d) Agility
e) Self-organization
f) Cross-functionality

85. What is the purpose of the Sprint Retrospective? Select three answers.
a) Identify and order the major items that went well and potential improvements
b) Create a plan for implementing improvements to the way the Scrum Team does its work
c) Get feedback from the key stakeholders invited by the Product Owner
d) Inspect how the last Sprint went with regards to people, relationships, process and tools
e) Get technical or domain advice from specialists invited by the Development Team or the Scrum Master

86. What could be a source of requirements for any changes to be made to the product?
a) Key stakeholders
b) CEO of the organization
c) Product Backlog

87. Who participates in the Sprint Review? Select all possible answers.
a) Development Team
b) Scrum Master
c) Key stakeholders
d) Product Owner
e) Organization CEO

88. What is the Sprint Retrospective?
a) It is a meeting to inspect the increment and adapt the Product Backlog if needed
b) It is the key inspect and adapt meeting
c) It is a meeting where the Development Team synchronizes activities and creates a plan for the next 24 hours
d) It is an opportunity for the Scrum Team to inspect itself and create a plan for improvements to be enacted during the next Sprint

6.4. Sample Exam Answers

1. d) The Development Team
2. a) It should have all competencies needed to accomplish the work without depending on others not part of the team
   b) It should choose how best to accomplish their work, rather than being directed by others outside the team
3. b) False
4. a) Scrum Master
5. a) Openness
   b) Courage
   c) Commitment
   e) Focus
   f) Respect
6. a) Product Owner
   b) Development Team
   c) Scrum Master
7. b) True
8. b) Product Owner
9. b) How much is known about the product over time
10. a) Ensures that the Development Team has the meeting
    c) Teaches the Development Team to keep the Daily Scrum within the 15-minute timebox

        d) If others are present at the Daily Scrum the Scrum Master ensures that they do not disrupt the meeting
11.   d) Sprint Planning
      b) Daily Scrum
      a) Sprint Review
      c) Sprint Retrospective
12.   a) Definition of Done guides the Development Team in knowing how many Product Backlog items it can select during a Sprint Planning
      b) Definition of Done ensures artifact transparency
      d) Definition of Done is used to assess when work is complete on the product increment
13.   c) Empiricism
14.   a) Lead facilitator of key stakeholder involvement
      b) Product value maximizer
      e) Product marketplace expert
15.   b) Development Team
16.   a) Make sure the Sprint Backlog for the next Sprint includes at least one high priority process improvement.
17.   all answers are correct
18.   b) Creativity
      c) Flexibility
      d) Productivity
19.   Sprint Review d) 4 hours or less
      Sprint Planning c) 8 hours or less
      Daily Scrum b) 15 minutes
      Sprint Retrospective a) 3 hours or less

20. a) As long as a product exists, its Product Backlog also exists
b) It is dynamic
c) It is never complete
21. a) How much work remains till the end of the sprint
22. c) Product Owner
23. b) False
24. a) True
25. e) Complex work that can include all the suggested options and even more
26. a) Scrum Master
27. a) False
28. d) Development Team
29. a) A small team of people that is highly flexible and adaptive
30. a) Understanding product planning in an empirical environment
b) Facilitating Scrum events as requested or needed
c) Finding techniques for effective Product Backlog management
31. b) False
32. a) The Development Team but with permission of the Product Owner
b) The Product Owner
33. a) False
34. b) Optimizing the value of the work the Development Team performs

c) Ensuring that the Product Backlog is visible, transparent and clear to all and shows what the Scrum Team will work on next

e) Ordering the items in the Product Backlog to best achieve goals and missions

35. a) Sprint Review
 c) Sprint Planning
36. c) The Product Backlog items selected for this Sprint plus the plan for delivering them
37. b) False
38. a) Scrum recognizes no titles for Development Team members other than Developer
 b) Scrum recognizes no sub-teams in the Development Team
 d) Accountability belongs to the Development Team as a whole
39. a) False
40. c) The Product Backlog items selected for this Sprint plus the plan for delivering them
41. a) Frequently, but it should not get in the way of the work
42. a) 2 teams of 6 and 4 people (the professionals after a short meeting decided this is the best option)
 d) 3 teams of 4, 3 and 3 people (each team is cross-functional)
43. a) Scrum Team
44. c) Less valuable and most unclear items at the bottom
45. b) False

46. a) Coaching the Development Team in self-organization and cross-functionality
b) Removing impediments to the Development Team's progress
d) Helping the Development Team to create high-value products
47. b) A revised Product Backlog that defines the probable Product Backlog items for the next Sprint
48. a) Daily Scrum
b) Sprint Planning
c) Sprint Retrospective
e) Sprint Review
49. c) The sum of all the Product Backlog items completed during the Sprint and the value of the increments of all previous Sprints
50. a) False
51. b) False
52. a) Not more than 8 hours
53. a) The latest product increment
b) Projected capacity of the Development Team during the Sprint
c) The Product Backlog
d) Past performance of the Development Team
54. b) False
55. a) Definition of Done of other Scrum Teams working on the same product
b) Conventions, standards and guidelines of the organization
56. b) Yes

57. c) Product Owner
58. b) True
59. a) Development Team
60. b) False
61. a) Planning Scrum implementations within the organization
    c) Leading and coaching the organization in the Scrum adoption
    e) Working with other Scrum Masters to increase the effectiveness of the application of Scrum in the organization
62. a) Quality goals do not decrease
    b) No changes are made that would endanger the Sprint Goal
    d) Scope may be clarified and re-negotiated between the Product Owner and Development Team as more is learned
63. a) All incomplete Product Backlog items are re-estimated and put back on the Product Backlog
    b) If part of the work is potentially releasable the Product Owner typically accepts it
    c) Any completed and "Done" Product Backlog items are reviewed
64. a) Do I see any impediment that prevents me or the Development Team from meeting the Sprint Goal?
    b) What did I do yesterday that helped the Development Team meet the Sprint Goal?
    d) What will I do today to help the Development Team meet the Sprint Goal?

65. b) Sprint Backlog
66. a) False
67. a) False
68. d) Sprint Goal
69. b) No
70. b) Sprint Review
71. c) Development Team
72. a) A framework within which people can address complex adaptive problems, while delivering valuable products
73. b) What ca be delivered in the Increment resulting from the upcoming Sprint?
    c) How will the work needed to deliver the Increment be achieved
74. a) Increment
    b) Sprint Backlog
    c) Product Backlog
75. a) As soon as possible to minimize further deviation
76. a) Scrum Master
    b) Product Owner
    c) Development Team
77. c) Not more than 10%
78. b) True
79. b) True
80. b) Product Owner
81. a) Events
    d) Roles
    e) Rules
    f) Artifacts

82. b) Yes, if the remaining work is also estimated, maybe in bigger units
83. a) Development Team
84. a) Transparency
b) Inspection
c) Adaption
85. a) Identify and order the major items that went well and potential improvements
b) Create a plan for implementing improvements to the way the Scrum Team does its work
d) Inspect how the last Sprint went with regards to people, relationships, process and tools
86. c) Product Backlog
87. a) Development Team
b) Scrum Master
c) Key stakeholders
d) Product Owner
88. d) It is an opportunity for the Scrum Team to inspect itself and create a plan for improvements to be enacted during the next Sprint

www.ingramcontent.com/pod-product-compliance
Lightning Source LLC
Chambersburg PA
CBHW021443210526
45463CB00002B/623